I0015201

MICROSOFT COPILOT

Step-by-Step Tutorial for Harnessing the Power of Advanced Features to Revolutionize Your Workflow and Boost Productivity.

INKGENIUS PRESS

COPYRIGHT PAGE

All rights reserved. No part of this publication may be reproduced, distributed, or transmitted in any form or by any means, including photocopying, recording, or other electronic or mechanical methods, without the prior written permission of the publisher, except in the case of brief quotations embodied in critical reviews and certain other noncommercial uses permitted by copyright law.

Copyright © (INKGENIUS PRESS), (2024).

Table of contents

Chapter 1: Introduction to Copilot

Imagine a world where coding feels like a collaborative effort, where your ideas seamlessly transform into lines of powerful code with the help of an AI assistant. Microsoft Copilot is that tireless assistant, fluent in the language of technology, always ready to complete your thoughts and translate them into code. This book is your key to unlocking Copilot's full potential. Whether you're an experienced developer or just starting out, Copilot can revolutionize your approach to software creation.

When you're stuck debugging, Copilot analyzes your code, pinpointing potential errors and suggesting fixes, saving you hours of frustration. If you're staring at a blank page, Copilot understands your intentions, generating relevant code snippets and entire functions based on your prompts, jumpstarting your creativity. And if repetitive tasks drain your energy, Copilot automates the mundane, filling in boilerplate code so you can focus on the innovative aspects of your project.

This book goes beyond the basics, exploring into Copilot's advanced capabilities and unlocking a world of possibilities. You'll learn how to craft powerful prompts that guide Copilot toward your desired outcome, master advanced techniques like code completion and refactoring, and even customize Copilot to seamlessly integrate into your workflow. But Copilot isn't just a productivity tool. This book also explores the ethical considerations of using AI in coding, ensuring you use Copilot responsibly and avoid pitfalls like plagiarism.

Real-world case studies showcase how developers leverage Copilot to achieve remarkable results. You'll learn from their successes and failures, gaining valuable insights into maximizing your own Copilot experience. This book is your roadmap to a future where coding becomes a collaborative effort between you and Copilot. Together, you'll push the boundaries of creativity, efficiency, and innovation in software development.

Are you ready to embark on this exciting journey with Copilot? Open this book and unlock the code to a brighter future.

What is Copilot and how does it work?

In the fast-paced world of software development, efficiency and innovation are crucial. Microsoft Copilot aims to revolutionize this field by acting as an intelligent coding partner for developers of all levels. But what exactly is Copilot, and how does it work its magic behind the scenes?

Introducing Copilot: Your AI Code Collaborator

Imagine having a coding partner who anticipates your needs, understands your programming language, and offers suggestions to streamline your workflow. This is the core function of Copilot. This AI-powered tool seamlessly integrates into your development environment, analyzing your code and offering contextually relevant suggestions in real-time. Think of it as an assistant constantly observing and assisting you in crafting efficient, well-structured code.

The Inner Workings of Copilot: Unveiling the Technology

Copilot leverages the power of machine learning, specifically a technique called "code completion." This technique involves training complex algorithms on vast amounts of existing code. These algorithms then learn to identify patterns and predict the most likely continuation of a code sequence based on the current context.

Simplified breakdown of Copilot's operation:

1. Understanding Your Context: Copilot constantly monitors your coding activity, analyzing the syntax, variables, and overall structure of your code.

2. Predicting the Next Step: Based on this understanding, Copilot utilizes its trained models to predict the most probable code snippets that would logically complete your current line or function.

3. Offering Suggestions: Copilot presents these predicted code segments as suggestions, allowing you to accept, modify, or discard them at your discretion.

Beyond Prediction: The Power of Customization

Copilot doesn't just offer pre-built suggestions; it can adapt to your unique coding style and preferences. You can fine-tune its behavior by adjusting settings related to:

Language and Framework: Specify the programming language and framework you're working with, allowing Copilot to tailor its suggestions accordingly.

Code Style: Define your preferred coding style, including indentation, spacing, and naming conventions, ensuring Copilot aligns with your coding standards.

Suggestion Level: Control the level of detail in Copilot's suggestions, ranging from complete function or class definitions to smaller code snippets.

By leveraging these customization options, you can personalize Copilot's assistance to seamlessly blend with your workflow and coding habits.

The Rewards of Copiloting Your Development

Enhanced Productivity: Automation of repetitive tasks and code completion capabilities significantly reduce development time, allowing you to focus on the more creative aspects of coding.

Improved Code Quality: Copilot helps identify potential errors and suggests best practices, leading to cleaner, more maintainable code.

Reduced Cognitive Load: By suggesting relevant code snippets, Copilot frees up your mental space, allowing you to focus on the overall logic and structure of your program.

Learning Through Collaboration: Working with Copilot exposes you to different coding styles and techniques, potentially leading to an expansion of your coding knowledge.

A New Era of Development: The Future with Copilot

Microsoft Copilot represents a significant leap forward in the realm of coding tools. By offering intelligent suggestions and seamlessly integrating into your development environment, it empowers developers to write cleaner, more efficient code while fostering innovation and creativity. Whether you're a seasoned developer or just starting your coding journey, Copilot can be a valuable companion, helping you navigate the ever-evolving landscape of software development.

Benefits of using Copilot

In today's world of software creation, efficiency and innovation are crucial. Microsoft Copilot emerges as a powerful tool designed to empower developers of all levels by acting as their intelligent coding partner. But beyond the initial introduction, what are the tangible benefits of utilizing Copilot in your development process? Let's explore the key advantages that can significantly enhance your coding experience.

Boosting Productivity

Imagine streamlining your coding workflow by automating repetitive tasks and receiving real-time code completion suggestions. Copilot does precisely that, significantly reducing development time. Instead of manually typing out boilerplate code or getting stuck searching for the right syntax, Copilot helps you move forward quickly, allowing you to focus on the more critical aspects of coding, like problem-solving and implementing complex logic.

This translates to a notable increase in overall productivity, enabling you to achieve more within a shorter timeframe.

Elevating Code Quality:

Maintaining clean and well-structured code is vital for ensuring the smooth operation and future maintainability of your projects. Copilot acts as your coding companion, proactively identifying potential errors and suggesting best practices. This includes suggesting proper syntax, variable naming conventions, and code formatting styles that adhere to established coding standards. By leveraging

Copilot's assistance, you can significantly reduce the risk of introducing errors and ensure your code is not only functional but also easy to understand and work with in the future, both for yourself and other developers collaborating on the project.

Reducing Cognitive Load:

Coding can be mentally demanding, requiring you to juggle complex logic, syntax rules, and various technical details. Copilot helps alleviate this cognitive load by acting as a suggestive tool. It analyzes your code in real-time, understanding the context and offering relevant code snippets that could potentially complete your current line or function. This reduces the mental strain of constantly searching for the right syntax or remembering specific code structures, allowing you to focus on the bigger picture – the overall design and functionality of your program.

Fostering Continuous Learning:

Learning new coding languages, frameworks, and best practices can be a continuous process. Copilot presents a unique opportunity to learn and expand your coding knowledge through everyday development tasks. As you work alongside Copilot, you are exposed to different coding styles, syntax variations, and potential solutions that may not have been familiar to you before. This continuous exposure to diverse coding practices can act as a catalyst for learning and skill development, helping you broaden your knowledge base and become a more versatile developer.

Encouraging Collaboration and Innovation:

While Copilot serves as an individual coding companion, its benefits extend to collaborative development environments as well. By offering standardized and consistent code completion suggestions, Copilot helps ensure a cohesive coding style within a team, even if individual developers have slightly different coding preferences.

This can streamline the collaboration process and improve code maintainability when multiple developers are working on the same project. Additionally, Copilot's ability to suggest various solutions and coding approaches can spark innovative discussions within development teams, leading to new ideas and creative problem-solving techniques.

By understanding these key benefits, it becomes clear that Copilot transcends a simple code suggestion tool. It becomes a valuable partner in your development journey, offering practical assistance, fostering continuous learning, and promoting collaboration, ultimately propelling you towards writing more efficient, high-quality code and paving the way for innovative software creation.

System requirements and compatibility

Microsoft Copilot, the AI-powered coding assistant, promises to revolutionize development workflows. But before you dive into its potential, it's crucial to assess compatibility and ensure your system meets the necessary requirements.

Operating System:

Windows: Copilot is primarily available for Windows 11, offering users a robust coding experience. However, Microsoft is gradually rolling it out to additional markets, so stay tuned for updates if you're using a different operating system.

Other Operating Systems: While not officially supported at the moment, Microsoft might explore compatibility with other operating systems in the future, expanding accessibility to a broader user base.

Hardware:

Processing Power: Smooth operation of Copilot demands a capable processor. While Microsoft hasn't specified minimum or recommended specs, opting for a mid-range or high-end processor from recent generations is advisable for optimal performance.

Memory (RAM): Efficient multitasking and data handling are facilitated by sufficient RAM. Aim for at least 8GB of RAM, with 16GB or more recommended, particularly if you work with large codebases or resource-intensive applications alongside Copilot.

Storage: While Copilot itself doesn't consume significant storage space, ensure you have ample storage available for your development environment and code projects, catering to your typical needs.

Software:

Microsoft 365: Copilot is currently available as an add-on for specific Microsoft 365 plans, including E3, E5, A5, and Business Standard/Premium. Note that individual and perpetual license users of Office 365 are not currently eligible for Copilot access.

Microsoft Entrap ID: Access to Copilot requires a Microsoft Entrap ID account, granting users access to compatible Microsoft 365 apps and services such as Word, Excel, PowerPoint, and others.

Application Compatibility: Copilot's functionality may vary depending on the application in use. Refer to Microsoft's official documentation for details on supported applications and their individual functionalities.

Microsoft 365 Apps Update Channel: To ensure seamless compatibility with Copilot, ensure your Microsoft 365 apps are on the Current Channel or Monthly Enterprise Channel, adjusting settings as needed through your organization's IT department or your Microsoft 365 admin center.

Additional Considerations:

Internet Connection: While Copilot primarily functions offline, an internet connection is necessary for initial setup, activation, and downloading updates, ensuring you stay current with the latest enhancements.

Supported Languages: Presently, Copilot predominantly supports English language input and code generation, catering to a diverse range of developers.

Staying Informed:

Microsoft is committed to continuous development and updates for Copilot, potentially leading to evolving system requirements and compatibility. Stay abreast of the latest information and potential changes by regularly consulting Microsoft's official documentation and announcements.

By understanding and meeting these requirements, you can prepare your system for seamless Copilot integration, unlocking its potential to elevate your coding experience.

Microsoft Copilot stands as a potent ally for developers, promising to streamline workflows and amplify coding efficiency. This AI-powered assistant analyzes your code in real-time, offering relevant completions and aiding in various tasks. However, before delving into the realm of Copilot-powered development, setting it up correctly is paramount. This guide will navigate you through the simple process of initiating Copilot, ensuring you harness its capabilities to the fullest.

<u>Essential Requirements:</u>

To harness Copilot's prowess, ensure you meet these fundamental prerequisites:

1. Compatible Development Environment: Copilot seamlessly integrates with several leading development environments, including Visual Studio Code, Visual Studio, and select web-based editors. Confirm you're using a compatible environment for smooth integration.

2. Eligible Microsoft 365 Subscription: Not all Microsoft 365 subscriptions include Copilot. You'll require a plan that explicitly provides access, such as Microsoft 365 E5 or a standalone Copilot for Microsoft 365 license.

3. Stable Internet Connection: Copilot relies on internet connectivity to access its AI models and deliver suggestions. Guarantee a reliable internet connection for optimal performance.

Installation and Setup:

While specifics may vary slightly based on your chosen development environment, the general installation and configuration steps encompass:

1. Accessing the Extension Store: Within your development environment, locate the extension store or marketplace. Search for "Microsoft Copilot" and install the official extension.

2. Sign in and Activation: Upon installation, initiate Copilot and sign in using your Microsoft account linked to your eligible Microsoft 365 subscription. This step activates Copilot, granting access to its features.

3. Customization (Optional): Though not obligatory, Copilot offers customization options to align with your preferences. Customize settings related to language, framework, code style, and suggestion level to tailor Copilot's behavior to your liking.

Navigating Copilot's Interface:

Once set up, Copilot seamlessly integrates into your development environment. As you commence coding, contextual suggestions will appear as you type, encompassing:

Code Completions: Predicting the most probable code continuations based on your context, Copilot suggests variable names, function calls, or entire code blocks.

Alternative Implementations: Offering alternative methods to achieve identical functionality, Copilot presents additional options for consideration.

Documentation Snippets: Providing relevant documentation snippets for specific functions or libraries aids in understanding and usage.

Interacting with Copilot:

To leverage Copilot's suggestions effectively:

Accept Suggestions: Utilize the Tab key or mouse to select and automatically insert desired suggestions into your code.

Modify Suggestions: Edit suggested code before acceptance to align with your specific requirements.

Reject Suggestions: Dismiss unhelpful suggestions by ignoring or using the Escape key.

Pro Tips:

Clear Contextual Input: Enhance the accuracy and relevance of Copilot's suggestions by providing comprehensive information in your code, including comments and variable names.

Experiment and Discover: Explore various settings and suggestions to uncover Copilot's optimal assistance for your development style.

Remember Copilot's Role: While Copilot offers valuable support, it complements rather than replaces your coding expertise and judgment. Always review and understand code before integrating it into your project.

By adhering to these steps and acquainting yourself with Copilot's functionalities, you can efficiently set up and harness this potent AI tool to elevate your coding journey, bolster efficiency, and ignite innovation in your software development endeavors.

Installation and configuration for different applications (Word, Excel, Teams, Visual Studio Code, etc.)

Welcome to the realm of Microsoft Copilot, your trusted AI companion in the world of coding. Before you soar into the boundless possibilities it offers, let's navigate through the setup process tailored for different software environments

1. Setting Sail with Copilot in Visual Studio Code (VS Code):

VS Code, a favored code editor, seamlessly integrates with Copilot. Here's your roadmap:

Installation: Launch VS Code and head to the Extensions tab (in on Windows/Linux, in on Mac). Search for "GitHub Copilot" and install the official extension.

Configuration: Once installed, restart VS Code. Follow the prompts to sign in with your GitHub account, essential for unlocking Copilot's features. Customize settings like code style and suggestion level within the VS Code settings menu to tailor Copilot to your preferences.

2. Empowering Your Writing in Microsoft Word:

Elevate your writing experience with Copilot's support in Word:

Availability: Copilot for Microsoft 365, inclusive of Word integration, is accessible as a premium add-on for select Microsoft 365 subscriptions. Consult your administrator or visit the Microsoft 365 admin center for subscription details.

Deployment: If Copilot for Microsoft 365 is part of your organization's subscription, your administrator will oversee deployment. Keep an eye out for a notification once it's activated for your account.

3. Amplifying Collaboration in Microsoft Teams:

Fuel your team's synergy with Copilot's integration in Teams:

Availability: Similar to Word, Copilot's presence in Teams requires the Copilot for Microsoft 365 add-on and administrative deployment.

Activation: Upon deployment by your administrator, Copilot features will enrich Teams chats and channels, providing valuable suggestions for emails, meeting summaries, and other textual exchanges.

4. Simplifying Data Management with Microsoft Excel:

While not yet standalone, Copilot's anticipated integration within Excel is forthcoming as part of the Copilot for Microsoft 365 suite. Stay tuned for updates and announcements from Microsoft.

5. Venturing into Additional Integrations:

Beyond the mentioned applications, Copilot is evolving to integrate with various other software and platforms. Keep a lookout on official Microsoft channels for updates on compatibility expansions.

Important Considerations:

Copilot's setup may vary slightly depending on your software version and operating system. Always refer to the official documentation for the latest guidance.

Not all Microsoft 365 applications may currently support Copilot. Consult Microsoft for a definitive list of supported applications within the Copilot for Microsoft 365 offering.

By following these navigational aids and staying abreast of developments, you'll be primed to harness Copilot's capabilities across diverse applications, transforming your workflow and unlocking boundless creative potential.

Activating and managing Copilot settings

Dive into the world of Microsoft Copilot, your AI-powered coding companion, designed to streamline your programming endeavors. To unlock its full potential, mastering the activation and management of Copilot's settings is crucial. This guide provides you with the insights needed to customize Copilot to align with your unique coding preferences and workflow.

Kickstarting Your Copilot Journey

Embarking on your Copilot journey varies across different platforms. Here's how to get started on the most popular ones:

Visual Studio Code:

1. Navigate to the Extensions tab in Visual Studio Code.

2. Type "GitHub Copilot" in the search bar and hit install.

3. post-installation, you'll be prompted to log in to your GitHub account to activate your Copilot trial or subscription.

Other IDEs:

For activating Copilot in other IDEs like JetBrains and Neo vim, refer to the official GitHub Copilot documentation for detailed instructions.

Customizing Copilot Settings: Enhancing Your Coding Experience

With Copilot activated, dive into its settings to fine-tune its behavior according to your needs. Here's a rundown of essential settings to consider:

Core Settings:

Copilot Activation: Easily switch Copilot on or off as per your requirement.

Inline Suggestions: Decide if you want Copilot to show suggestions directly in your editor or if you prefer activating them manually with keyboard shortcuts.

Programming Language: Define the language you're coming in, so Copilot can provide language-specific suggestions.

Visual Theme: Choose between light or dark themes for Copilot's suggestions to match your coding environment.

Advanced Customization:

Completion Detail: Adjust the level of detail in Copilot's suggestions, from full-function completions to smaller code snippets.

Data Privacy: Control how your coding data is used by Copilot. opt for limited data sharing while still benefiting from Copilot's assistance.

Shortcut Customization: Tailor the keyboard shortcuts for Copilot suggestions to fit your coding habits.

Further Tips:

License Management: For teams, explore options in the Microsoft 365 admin center for managing Copilot licenses and settings across the organization.

Community Insights: Leverage the wealth of information in the official GitHub Copilot documentation and online forums to discover tips and best practices.

Crafting a Personalized Copilot Experience

By taking control of Copilot's settings, you can mold it into an intuitive coding ally that syncs perfectly with your coding style and project demands. Keep in mind, the optimal settings may differ based on your personal coding approach, project needs, and comfort level with automation. Experiment with various configurations to pinpoint the perfect balance that enhances your coding efficiency and creativity, transforming Copilot into an indispensable partner in your software development journey.

Integrating Copilot with your development workflow

In the dynamic world of software development, efficiency reigns supreme. Developers are always on the lookout for tools and techniques that not only streamline their workflow but also provide the freedom to focus on the art of coding. Microsoft Copilot stands out as a game-changer in this context, offering an intelligent coding assistant that effortlessly melds with your development ecosystem. This guide delves into how you can seamlessly weave Copilot into your daily coding practice, unlocking its full potential to elevate your programming experience.

Deciphering Your Workflow and Requirements

The journey to harmonizing Copilot with your workflow begins with a deep dive into your current development practices. This entails pinpointing the repetitive or time-consuming tasks and understanding the nuances of your preferred tools and coding habits.

Consider the following:

Your Go-To Development Tools: Whether you swear by a specific Integrated Development Environment (IDE) like Visual Studio Code or a blend of a text editor and compiler, Copilot is designed to integrate smoothly with your tool of choice.

Coding Style and Preferences: Each developer has a unique approach to coding, from indentation and formatting to naming conventions. Copilot's adaptability ensures it can align with your personal coding style, making its suggestions feel like a natural extension of your thought process.

 Routine Coding Tasks: Identify the tasks that tend to eat up your time, such as crafting boilerplate code or implementing common data structures. These are areas where Copilot can step in and make a significant impact.

Integrating Copilot: Tailoring It to Your Coding Environment

With a clear understanding of your workflow, you can move on to embedding Copilot into your development environment. Most modern IDEs offer a straightforward setup for the Copilot extension. Once in place, take some time to tweak the settings to make Copilot truly yours.

Key settings to focus on include:

 Language and Framework Preferences: Inform Copilot about the programming language and framework you're using, enabling it to provide contextually relevant code completions and suggestions.

Code Style Adjustments: Fine-tune Copilot to adhere to your coding style preferences, covering aspects such as spacing, indentation, and naming conventions.

Customizing Suggestions: Tailor the granularity of Copilot's suggestions, from comprehensive function definitions to concise code snippets, based on your needs and the task complexity.

Maximizing Copilot's Capabilities for Increased Productivity

With Copilot finely integrated and customized, you're set to explore the myriad ways it can enhance your coding efficiency. Here's how you can leverage Copilot's prowess:

Code Completion: Copilot's real-time suggestions for variables, functions, and code blocks can significantly cut down the time spent on routine coding and syntax lookups.

Refactoring Aid: When it's time to refactor, Copilot can offer alternative code structures and best practice recommendations, ensuring your code remains clean and efficient.

Contextual Suggestions: Copilot's intelligence shines in providing suggestions that are not just generic but tailored to the specific context of your project, including relevant variable names and function calls.

Adaptive Learning: As you code, Copilot learns from your style and preferences, making its future suggestions even more aligned with your coding habits.

Beyond Streamlining: Unleashing Creativity and Innovation

Copilot's value extends beyond mere efficiency; it's a catalyst for creativity and innovation. By automating the mundane aspects of coding, it frees your mind to focus on strategic thinking and creative problem-solving.

Here are ways Copilot can inspire your creativity:

Encouraging Experimentation: With more time at your disposal, you can explore different coding strategies and experiment with new solutions.

Learning New Technologies: Use the time saved by Copilot to dive into new libraries and frameworks, broadening your technical horizons and fostering innovation.

Concentrating on Problem Solving: Shift your focus from repetitive coding tasks to the heart of your project - the core logic and problem-solving, leading to more inventive and effective solutions.

By integrating Copilot into your development process and harnessing its features to the fullest, you not only streamline your coding workflow but also open the doors to a world of creativity and innovation. Copilot is more than just a tool; it's a partner in your quest to craft cleaner, more efficient code, paving the way for the development of groundbreaking software solutions.

Microsoft Copilot has transformed the coding landscape, offering more than just its remarkable code completion and refactoring prowess. One of its standout features is the ability to draft both text and code, ushering in a new era of efficiency and creativity for developers across the board.

The Fusion of Text and Code: A Game-Changer for Developers

The modern development landscape demands a blend of technical skills and clear communication. From crafting thorough documentation to composing articulate emails, a developer's day is filled with textual tasks. Copilot steps in to bridge the gap, offering a unified platform for creating both text and code.

Maximizing Copilot's Textual Assistance

Picture this: you're tasked with writing detailed documentation for your latest project. Copilot can scrutinize your code, suggesting precise explanations and descriptions, cutting down the time you spend on documentation and allowing you to concentrate on refining your message for clarity.

Expanding Horizons: The Versatility of Text Drafting

Copilot's capabilities in text drafting go beyond just documentation. Here are some other areas where it shines:

Writing informative comments: Move away from generic comments and let Copilot suggest comprehensive explanations that clarify your code's purpose, logic, and behavior.

Explaining technical concepts in emails: When communicating with non-technical stakeholders, Copilot can assist in drafting clear and concise emails, ensuring your message is understood without resorting to jargon.

Creating task descriptions and meeting agendas: Simplify project management by using Copilot to generate well-organized task descriptions and agendas, highlighting essential information and action items.

Tailoring Your Textual Assistant to Your Needs

Copilot's text suggestions can be customized to suit your preferences, allowing you to:

Define the context: By providing context, you enable Copilot to generate suggestions that are more aligned with your text's purpose.

Choose your tone: Depending on your audience and the nature of your message, you can select a tone that's either formal or informal.

Refine suggestions: Copilot's suggestions are a starting point. Feel free to tweak them to match your communication style and the content you want to convey.

The Benefits of Integrating Text and Code

Embracing text drafting in your development process brings multiple advantages:

Increased Productivity: Save precious time by minimizing the manual effort involved in writing documentation, comments, and other textual elements.

Clearer Communication: Enhance the clarity and conciseness of your communication, both within your team and with external parties.

Enhanced Creativity: By exploring new ways to articulate your technical thoughts, you may unlock creative solutions and innovative approaches to problem-solving.

Embracing a Collaborative Approach with Copilot

Copilot's text-drafting feature emphasizes the collaborative nature of software development, which goes beyond mere coding. By integrating text and code creation seamlessly, Copilot enables developers to become more effective communicators, fostering efficient collaboration and sharing of ideas within their teams.

Unlocking Collaboration with Copilot

Whether you're an experienced developer or a newcomer, Copilot's text-drafting capabilities provide a powerful tool to enhance your workflow and communication skills. Dive into this unique feature and discover how it can streamline your development process, improve your communication, and inspire new levels of creativity and teamwork.

Providing effective prompts and instructions

Microsoft Copilot isn't just a coding tool; it's a collaborative partner poised to revolutionize your development workflow. To unlock its full potential, the key lies in mastering the art of communication. Effective prompts and instructions are your secret weapons, transforming your coding aspirations into copilot's actionable insights.

The Essence of Clear Communication:

Picture working with a colleague who speaks a different language. The collaboration would be fraught with misunderstandings. Similarly, Copilot needs clear guidance to understand your objectives, preventing irrelevant or off-target suggestions.

The Craft of Creating Compelling Prompts:

Prompts are the heart of your interaction with Copilot. They're like a compass, guiding Copilot's responses. Here's how to craft prompts that hit the mark:

Precision and Clarity: Steer clear of ambiguity. Rather than saying "enhance this code," pinpoint the exact enhancement you seek, such as a specific function or problem you're addressing.

Context Matters: Paint a vivid picture of your code's landscape and your project's ultimate goals. This helps Copilot grasp the bigger picture, leading to suggestions that resonate with your vision.

Illustrate with Examples: Wherever possible, sprinkle in code snippets or examples to crystallize your request. This sets a solid foundation for Copilot's suggestions.

Examples of Spot-On Prompts:

"Craft a function that accepts two numbers and returns their product."

"Develop code that displays a customized error message based on user input."

"Expand this code snippet to include a loop that traverses an array of items."

Refining Your Communication with Instructions:

While prompts lay the foundation, instructions build the structure. They offer Copilot a detailed blueprint of how to tackle your request. Here are some strategies for crafting instructions that resonate:

Action-Oriented Guidance: Move beyond generic requests like "correct this code." Specify the exact steps, such as renaming a variable for clarity or refining a function for performance.

Highlight Constraints: If your project has particular requirements or limitations, such as memory constraints or compatibility issues, make them known. This ensures Copilot's suggestions align with your project's unique specifications.

Incorporate External References: If relevant, point Copilot towards documentation or code examples that can further refine its understanding.

Examples of Impactful Instructions:

"Adopt meaningful variable names throughout the code."

"Align the code with the project's established style guidelines."

"Focus on enhancing the code's readability and maintainability."

Unlocking Copilot's Potential Through Communication:

By honing your skills in crafting precise prompts and instructions, you set the stage for Copilot to deliver its most valuable assistance. Remember, the more detailed and specific your communication, the more accurate and useful Copilot's suggestions will be, propelling you towards a more streamlined and effective development journey.

Understanding Copilot's suggestions and responses

Embark on a journey with Microsoft Copilot, your AI navigator in the coding universe. This digital co-pilot has redefined the coding landscape, offering real-time insights and solutions to enhance your coding voyage. Yet, mastering the art of interpreting and integrating Copilot's wisdom into your projects is akin to learning a new language. This guide serves as your compass, helping you decipher the language of Copilot, transforming its advice into invaluable assets for your coding endeavors.

1. The Map of Context:

Copilot's guidance is a treasure trove of insights, meticulously crafted from the map of your current code. The treasures it offers are influenced by:

The Current Code Line: Your current position, marked by the variables, functions, and syntax in use.

The Terrain of Surrounding Code: The landscape of code that surrounds your position, offering Copilot clues about the broader project goals and architecture.

The Dialect of Programming Language and Framework: The specific language and framework you're navigating, dictating the syntax and functionalities at your disposal.

With these elements, Copilot charts a course, aiming to predict and propose the most suitable paths forward in your coding journey.

2. Unearthing Suggestions:

Copilot's compass points you toward a variety of coding riches:

Code Completion Treasures: It unveils paths by completing functions, loops, or conditions, taking cues from the map of your code.

Hints to Hidden Variables and Functions: It suggests names or functions that resonate with the coding landscape, drawn from widespread libraries and practices.

Routes to Alternative Structures: Sometimes, Copilot reveals alternate trails to reach the same destination, offering you the choice of paths to follow.

3. Charting the Course:

These suggestions are beacons, not directives. Their true value is unlocked through careful scrutiny:

Accuracy Checkpoints: Validate the suggested route for syntax correctness, adherence to coding principles, and alignment with your project's logic.

Maintainability Markers: opt for paths that enhance code clarity, ease of reading, and future adaptability.

Personal Style Signposts: Ensure that the suggestions mirror your coding preferences and stylistic choices.

Exercising Your Navigator's Wisdom: Feel empowered to modify or navigate away from Copilot's suggestions if they don't align with your vision or if you discover more efficient routes.

4. Enhancing Dialogue with Your Digital Navigator:

Refining your interaction with Copilot is akin to honing your navigation skills:

Clarify Your Map: Employ comments and descriptive naming to clarify your intentions, making it easier for Copilot to guide you accurately.

Adjust the Compass: Tailor Copilot's settings to align with your preferred coding dialect, style, and landscape, ensuring its guidance is more attuned to your needs.

Embark on Learning Voyages: Engage with Copilot across various coding scenarios to understand its language better. Each interaction is an opportunity to learn how to interpret its suggestions more effectively.

By mastering the context of Copilot's guidance, evaluating its proposed paths with a critical eye, and refining your communication with this digital navigator, you unlock a powerful ally in your coding expeditions. Copilot is designed to assist, not to captain your journey. It invites you to embrace its insights as a rich resource, all the while steering your projects with your own expertise and vision.

Accepting, discarding, and regenerating suggestions

Step into the dance of coding with Microsoft Copilot, your AI choreographer, guiding you through the intricate steps of software development. But how do you lead in this dance, ensuring that Copilot follows your tempo? This guide delves into the essential techniques of embracing, setting aside, and reimagining Copilot's cues, transforming you from a mere participant to a maestro in the symphony of coding.

Embracing the Perfect Harmony: When Copilot Strikes the Right Chord

Picture yourself composing a function to calculate the area of a rectangle. You've laid down the framework and declared the essential variables. Now, it's time to pen the formula. Copilot, in tune with your rhythm, suggests the precise equation, `length width`. After a brief review, you recognize its accuracy and congruence with your context. Embracing this suggestion effortlessly completes your line of code, saving you valuable time and ensuring accuracy

However, embracing suggestions isn't always an automatic reflex. It's essential to:

Review for Precision: Scrutinize the suggested snippet for any potential discrepancies or conflicts with your existing code or logic.

Consider Clarity: Assess whether the suggestion harmonizes with your coding style and maintains readability for you and your collaborators.

Retain Ownership: Remember, you are the conductor of your code. Embracing a suggestion doesn't relieve you of the responsibility to comprehend its function.

The Grace of Releasing: When Copilot Falls Out of Step

Not every cue from Copilot will resonate with your coding melody. Reasons for releasing a suggestion can include:

Mismatched Functionality: The suggested code might not execute the intended action or could introduce errors into your code.

Irrelevant Context: The suggestion might be generally pertinent but not suited to the specific context of your current composition.

Style Dissonance: The suggestion might not align with your preferred coding style or the coding standards of your project.

When faced with an unsuitable suggestion, gracefully let it go. Click the "x" icon next to the suggestion or use the keyboard shortcuts provided by your development environment. This signals to Copilot that the suggestion is not in harmony and allows you to move on.

Reimagining for a Fresh Cadence: When You Seek a New Rhythm

At times, the initial suggestion might not fully align with your vision but could still inspire new directions. This is where the magic of reimagining comes into play. By clicking the "regenerate" icon or using the corresponding keyboard shortcut, you invite Copilot to present a new alternative suggestion. This can be invaluable when:

Exploring Diverse Pathways: You wish to examine various approaches to solving the problem at hand and compare different code structures.

Fine-tuning the Suggestion: You're close to the ideal solution but need a slight adjustment in the suggested code.

Breaking Creative Blocks: A fresh suggestion can dispel the fog of writer's block and provide a new starting point to advance.

Remember, reimagining doesn't erase the previous suggestion; it simply unveils another option alongside the existing one. You can then select the most suitable code snippet for your masterpiece.

By mastering the art of embracing, releasing, and reimagining Copilot's suggestions, you elevate this powerful tool from a mere code completion engine to an active collaborator. You orchestrate the flow of suggestions, ensuring they synchronize with your coding style, logic, and overarching project goals. This collaborative approach empowers you to craft cleaner, more efficient code while deepening your understanding of the coding process itself, all in perfect harmony with your AI partner.

Customizing Copilot's style and tone

Step into the realm of Microsoft Copilot, your intelligent coding ally, designed to offer real-time guidance as you craft your code. But what happens when Copilot's suggestions don't quite resonate with your unique coding flair or the specific ambiance your project demands? Fear not, for Copilot comes equipped with a plethora of customization options, enabling you to sculpt its suggestions to perfectly complement your coding style and the tone of your project.

Decoding Style and Tone in the World of Coding:

- Style: This encompasses the structural blueprint of your code, including the conventions you adhere to for indentation, spacing, naming variables, and commenting. A consistent style is more than just a cosmetic choice; it's a testament to your professionalism and commitment to best practices, ensuring that your code remains readable and maintainable.

- Tone: While more subtle than style, the tone of your code is about how it communicates with fellow developers. It's influenced by your choice of language (opting for descriptive variable names, for instance), the granularity of your comments, and the overall architecture of your code.

Personalizing Copilot for a Tailored Experience:

Copilot offers a suite of features to align its suggestions with your personal preferences and project requisites:

1. Language and Framework Preferences: By specifying the programming language and framework in use, you guide Copilot to generate suggestions that adhere to the syntax and conventions unique to your chosen language.

2. Code Style Customization: Set your preferences for indentation, spacing, and naming conventions, and watch as Copilot prioritizes suggestions that mirror your stylistic choices.

3. Suggestion Detail Control: Adjust the granularity of Copilot's suggestions to suit your needs, from complete function definitions to concise code snippets or variable names.

4. Contextual Clarity Through Comments: Enhance Copilot's understanding by annotating your code with clear comments, explaining the purpose of functions, logic, or design decisions. This ensures that Copilot's suggestions align with the broader context and tone of your project.

5. Refinement Through Interaction: Over time, as you interact with Copilot, it learns from your preferences. By accepting or adjusting suggestions, you subtly guide Copilot to better align with your desired style and tone.

The Rewards of a Custom-Fit Copilot:

Tailoring Copilot's behavior to your liking brings a host of benefits:

- Boosted Readability and Maintenance: A consistent style enhances the readability of your code, making it easier for you and your peers to navigate and maintain it over time.

- Minimized Refactoring: When Copilot's suggestions are in harmony with your style, you'll find yourself spending less time tweaking code to meet your stylistic standards.

- Elevated Communication: Clear, concise, and well-explained code fosters better collaboration and understanding among developers.

- Project-Specific Attunement: You can fine-tune Copilot's tone to reflect the objectives of your project, whether it's using detailed comments for public-facing code or opting for brevity in internal projects.

Dedicating time to customize Copilot transforms it from a mere tool to a true extension of your coding persona. By ensuring that its style and tone resonate with your preferences and the needs of your project, you unlock a powerful ally that not only streamlines your workflow but also elevates the clarity, maintainability, and collaborative potential of your code.

Microsoft Copilot has emerged as a trusted companion for developers, providing insightful code suggestions that streamline the coding process. But the true power of Copilot lies in its potential to be molded and enhanced. This guide delves into advanced Copilot techniques that can take your coding prowess to new heights.

1. Crafting the Perfect Guide: The Art of Precise Prompts:

The magic of Copilot unfolds when you provide clear, specific instructions. Imagine your prompts as a detailed map for Copilot to follow. Here's how to chart a precise course:

Detail is Your Friend: The more detailed your prompt, the more tailored Copilot's suggestions will be. For instance, instead of a generic "sort this list," specify the sorting algorithm and data type for a more targeted response.

Set the Scene: Give Copilot a glimpse of the bigger picture. Providing context about your code's overarching purpose helps Copilot align its suggestions with your broader goals.

Build on What Exists: If you've already started coding a particular functionality, include that in your prompt. This serves as a reference point, aiding Copilot in crafting suggestions that seamlessly blend with your existing work.

2. Beyond Simple Suggestions: Unleashing Copilot's Full Potential:

Copilot's capabilities extend far beyond mere code completion. Harness its power to generate complete functions, classes, and even intricate data structures:

Automate with Function Factories: Streamline the creation of new functions by providing a descriptive name and purpose in your prompt. Copilot can conjure up the entire function definition, complete with parameters and basic logic.

Effortless Class Construction: Crafting a new class? Outline its purpose and key attributes in your prompt, and let Copilot handle the rest, generating a well-structured class skeleton for you.

3. Refining Your Code: Copilot's Assistance in Refactoring and Debugging:

Copilot is not just for writing new code; it's also a valuable ally in refining existing code:

Streamline with Refactoring: Share your current code and desired improvements with Copilot. It can suggest alternative implementations or restructuring techniques to enhance your code's readability and efficiency.

Debugging Insights: While not a substitute for thorough testing, Copilot can offer insights into potential errors. Describe the issue and the unexpected behavior, and Copilot might pinpoint the problem or suggest fixes.

4. Exploring Uncharted Territories: Copilot's Advanced Features:

Discover the array of advanced features Copilot offers:

Efficient Code Search: Quickly locate specific code segments within your project or public repositories using Copilot's search function. Need a summary of existing code? Copilot can provide a concise overview, shedding light on its purpose and implementation.

Tailor-Made Experience: Customize Copilot to align with your coding habits and workflow. Adjust settings related to code style, suggestion level, and language support to ensure Copilot feels like a natural extension of your coding process.

A Word of Caution: While Copilot is a formidable tool, it's crucial to review its suggestions critically. Adapt and scrutinize its recommendations to ensure they align with your coding standards and project requirements.

By embracing these advanced techniques, you can transform Copilot from a mere coding assistant into a dynamic partner, empowering you to write cleaner, more efficient code and navigate your coding journey with newfound speed and precision.

Leveraging Copilot for specific programming languages and frameworks

Embark on a journey with Microsoft Copilot, your AI-infused coding ally, as it transforms the landscape of software development. Renowned for its real-time code analysis and insightful suggestions, Copilot's true prowess lies in its adaptability. This guide will navigate you through the process of customizing Copilot to harness its full potential across a spectrum of programming languages and frameworks, ensuring a seamless and enriched coding experience.

Discovering Copilot's Core Strengths:

At the heart of Copilot's capabilities are its:

Contextual Predictions: It intricately analyzes syntax, variables, and code structure to offer logical completions and suggestions.

Learning from a Wealth of Code: Trained on a vast array of public code repositories, Copilot absorbs common patterns and best practices specific to each language and framework.

Personalization: You can fine-tune Copilot's behavior by setting your preferred language, framework, and coding style, ensuring its suggestions resonate with your coding ethos.

Unlocking the Potential in Various Languages:

Each programming language and framework comes with its distinct characteristics. Here's how Copilot can be fine-tuned to enhance your coding journey:

1. Python:

Function and Class Completions: Copilot shines in suggesting complete Python function definitions and class structures, particularly for popular libraries like NumPy and Pandas.

Automatic Docstring Generation: Utilize Copilot to generate comprehensive docstrings, leveraging Python's type hints to enhance code readability and maintainability.

2. JavaScript:

Framework-Specific Assistance: Whether you're using React, Angular, or Vue.js, Copilot can provide relevant suggestions for component structures, lifecycle methods, and integration with specific libraries.

Mastering Asynchronous Programming: Copilot aids in navigating the intricacies of promises and async/await syntax, offering snippets for error handling and chained operations.

3. Java:

Integration with Spring Framework: For Spring Boot enthusiasts, Copilot understands common Spring annotations, suggesting controller methods, service implementations, and dependency injection configurations.

Embracing Java 8 Features: Copilot is well-versed in Java 8 features like lambda expressions and functional interfaces, helping you streamline your code with functional programming techniques.

4. C#:

.NET Framework Insights: Copilot provides tailored suggestions for .NET libraries and frameworks, such as ASP.NET and Entity Framework, aiding in the development of desktop applications and web services.

Guidance on Async/Await: Copilot assists with asynchronous programming in C#, suggesting code for asynchronous methods and managing cancellation tasks.

Leveraging Framework-Specific Capabilities:

Copilot's versatility extends to frameworks, offering tailored assistance for:

Machine Learning Frameworks (TensorFlow, Porch): Get guidance on building neural network architectures, data preprocessing, and training loops.

Web Development Frameworks (Django, Express.js): Receive suggestions for routing, data models, and database interactions.

Optimizing Your Copilot Experience:

To fully unlock Copilot's potential:

Offer Rich Context: The more detailed context you provide through comments and variable names, the better Copilot can tailor its suggestions to your project's needs.

Tweak Settings: Explore and adjust language settings, code style preferences, and suggestion detail levels to align Copilot's behavior with your coding style and project requirements.

Leverage as a Learning Resource: Critically analyze Copilot's suggestions, delve into the logic behind them, and use them as a springboard to expand your coding knowledge.

By mastering Copilot's customization, you can transform it into a dynamic coding partner, adept at navigating the nuances of various programming languages and frameworks. Embrace Copilot's intelligent guidance, and elevate your coding efficiency and creativity to unparalleled heights.

Utilizing Copilot for code completion, refactoring, and debugging

In the ever-evolving realm of software development, the quest for efficiency and innovation is paramount. Enter Microsoft Copilot, your AI-infused coding companion, poised to revolutionize your coding adventures by guiding you towards crafting more elegant and robust code while unlocking your creative potential. Let's embark on an exploration of how Copilot can be your ally in three pivotal areas: code completion, refactoring, and debugging.

1. Code Completion: Setting Sail with Streamlined Development

Picture a co-navigator who anticipates your coding paths and presents you with a treasure trove of relevant suggestions as you chart your course. That's the essence of Copilot's code completion feature. As you begin to weave your code, Copilot delves into the context, analyzing variables, syntax, and the surrounding code tapestry. Armed with this insight, it predicts the most logical continuation of your current line, drawing from a wealth of established coding patterns.

These predictions are offered as suggestions, allowing you to effortlessly complete your code snippet, tailor them to your unique needs, or simply cast them aside and continue your coding journey. This feature not only accelerates your development voyage but also shifts your focus to the heart of your program's logic, enabling you to navigate through your coding journey with greater ease and efficiency.

2. Refactoring: Navigating Towards Improved Readability and Maintainability

As your codebase grows and winds through the complexities of development, maintaining its clarity and structure becomes a crucial endeavor. Here, Copilot emerges as a valuable guide in the art of refactoring, helping you restructure your code to enhance its readability, efficiency, and overall integrity.

Copilot assists in this transformative journey by:

Charting areas for improvement: It scans your code's landscape, pinpointing potential redundancies or inefficiencies and suggesting routes for optimization.

Proposing alternative pathways: Upon identifying an opportunity for enhancement, Copilot presents different approaches to achieve the same functionality with cleaner, more streamlined code.

Polishing code style and readability: Copilot can automatically format your code to align with your stylistic preferences, ensuring a visually coherent and easily navigable codebase.

By embracing Copilot's refactoring insights, you can ensure that your code remains organized, maintainable, and resilient, paving the way for smoother sailing in your development journey.

3. Debugging: Unearthing Errors with Precision and Speed

The task of debugging, a quest to uncover and rectify errors in your code, can often be a daunting and time-intensive endeavor. Copilot stands ready to expedite this process by offering a compass of insights and solutions:

Illuminating potential pitfalls: Leveraging its knowledge of coding best practices, Copilot can spotlight potential errors, urging you to investigate and rectify them proactively.

Providing solutions and explanations: Beyond merely identifying errors, Copilot suggests remedies and elucidates the underlying causes, reducing the time spent in the debugging labyrinth.

Simplifying intricate debugging quests: For complex debugging challenges, Copilot offers guidance through relevant documentation or suggests avenues for further exploration, aiding you in navigating through the maze of code to pinpoint the source of the error.

With Copilot's debugging prowess, you can swiftly navigate the waters of error resolution, allowing you to devote more time to crafting innovative software solutions.

In conclusion, Copilot emerges as a powerful ally in your coding odyssey, offering a suite of functionalities that not only streamline your development process but also elevate the quality of your code. Whether you're harnessing its code completion capabilities to expedite your coding voyage, utilizing its refactoring insights to maintain a pristine codebase, or relying on its debugging assistance to swiftly navigate through errors, Copilot stands as your intelligent coding companion, propelling you towards crafting superior software with newfound speed and creativity.

Exploring advanced features like code search and summarization

While Copilot's prowess in code completion is widely recognized, its capabilities extend far beyond crafting the next line of code. This robust tool harbors a treasure trove of advanced features, each designed to streamline your coding voyage and enrich your development experience.

1. Navigating the Codebase: The Art of Code Search

Embark on a journey through vast codebases with ease, thanks to Copilot's code search feature. Here's how it transforms your search experience:

Contextual Compass: Unlike traditional search tools, Copilot's code search delves into the context of your current code, offering a guided exploration rather than a mere keyword hunt.

Precision Mapping: Hone in on your target with intelligent filtering, specifying parameters like language, function name, or variable type to pinpoint exactly what you seek.

Integrated Journey: Access this search feature directly within your development environment, ensuring a seamless and uninterrupted coding journey.

The Rewards of Code Search:

Time-Saving Expeditions: Swiftly locate specific code elements, freeing up precious time for development.

Promoting Code Reuse: Unearth existing code that can be repurposed, fostering maintainability and reducing redundancy.

Deepening Codebase Understanding: Enhance your grasp of the project's structure and functionalities through exploratory searches.

2. Unveiling Complexity: The Power of Code Summarization

In the realm of intricate codebases, Copilot's code summarization feature shines as a beacon of clarity, offering succinct summaries of code sections, functions, or entire files.

The Mechanics of Summarization:

Effortless Extraction: Select the code in question, and Copilot distills its essence, highlighting key functionalities and logic.

Clear, Natural Language: The summaries are crafted in plain English, ensuring accessibility even for those with limited coding expertise.

Adaptable Detail: Tailor the summary's depth to your needs, from a broad overview to a detailed analysis of the code's purpose and functionality.

The Advantages of Code Summarization:

Enhanced Comprehension: Quickly grasp the core functions of complex code, bypassing the need for line-by-line deciphering.

Facilitating Collaboration: Communicate intricate code logic with ease to teammates or clients, fostering better project collaboration.

Streamlining Code Reviews: Identify potential issues or areas for improvement efficiently by understanding the foundational aspects of different code sections.

3. Personalizing the Experience: Advanced Customization Options

Copilot is not just a tool; it's your coding partner, offering customization options to align its assistance with your unique workflow and preferences.

- Language and Framework Preferences: Inform Copilot of the languages and frameworks you're using, ensuring its suggestions are tailored to your specific technological landscape.

Controlling Suggestion Detail: Adjust the granularity of Copilot's suggestions to suit your task, whether you need complete code snippets or just a hint.

Code Style Personalization: Define your coding style preferences, including formatting and naming conventions, and Copilot will incorporate these into its suggestions, maintaining consistency across your codebase.

By delving into Copilot's advanced features, you unlock a realm of possibilities, enhancing your development process with efficiency and clarity.

From effortlessly navigating codebases to understanding complex code structures, Copilot empowers you to conquer the challenges of software development with confidence and creativity.

Chapter 5: Working with Copilot in Different Applications

Microsoft Copilot has solidified its position as a valuable asset for developers looking to streamline their workflow and enhance their coding efficiency. Yet, its capabilities transcend the conventional Integrated Development Environment (IDE). Let's delve into how Copilot can harness its potential across diverse applications, empowering you to unlock its full capabilities.

Expanding Beyond Code Editors: Unveiling Copilot's Versatility

While Copilot excels in code editors like Visual Studio Code, its functionality extends beyond traditional development environments. Here's a glimpse into how Copilot can seamlessly integrate into various applications, amplifying your productivity and creativity:

1. Enhancing Team Communication:

- Effortless Email Crafting: When composing emails in platforms such as Microsoft Teams or Outlook, Copilot can assist in drafting concise and grammatically correct content. Picture receiving tailored suggestions for subject lines, body content, and professional greetings, all tailored to the recipient and context.

- Facilitating Meeting Agendas and Minutes: Crafting meeting agendas and minutes can be time-consuming. Copilot can analyze past meeting details and propose relevant talking points, action items, and attendees, saving you time and ensuring thorough documentation.

2. Boosting Documentation Efforts:

- Streamlined Content Creation: Whether creating user manuals, tutorials, or developer documentation, Copilot can suggest clear and concise language, ensuring your documentation is easily understood.

- Automating Repetitive Text: Many documents contain repetitive sections, such as disclaimers or copyright information. Copilot can learn and automate the insertion of these standard elements, freeing you to focus on unique content.

3. Improving Project Management:

- Simplified Task Breakdown: When outlining project plans in tools like Microsoft Project or Asana, Copilot can suggest appropriate task breakdowns and dependencies, ensuring your project roadmap is well-defined.

- Generating Meeting Notes and Action Items: During project meetings, Copilot can capture key discussions and automatically generate detailed notes, including action items with assigned individuals and deadlines, promoting clear communication and accountability.

4. Facilitating Data Analysis:

- Refined Query Formulation: Whether working with spreadsheets in Excel or exploring data visualization tools like Power BI, Copilot can assist in crafting precise and concise queries, enabling you to extract desired insights from your data sets efficiently.

- Generating Report Outlines and Summaries: When creating reports based on data analysis, Copilot can help structure outlines and suggest concise summaries of key findings, saving time and ensuring clarity in data presentation.

Unlocking Copilot's Potential: Tailoring to Your Needs

Copilot is designed to adapt and learn from your interactions. By consistently using it across different applications, you can train it to understand your specific needs and preferences, offering increasingly relevant suggestions and enhancing its effectiveness in diverse contexts.

Venturing beyond traditional coding, Copilot emerges as a powerful tool for boosting productivity and creativity across various applications. From communication to project management and data analysis, Copilot has the potential to revolutionize your workflow. Embrace its versatility and explore how it can empower you to achieve more in a range of applications.

Specific functionalities and workflows for Copilot in Word, Excel, Teams, and other applications

Microsoft Copilot, the AI-driven productivity tool, isn't confined to the realm of coding anymore. Its reach extends far beyond assisting with programming tasks, offering a wealth of functionalities across a spectrum of applications within the Microsoft 365 suite and beyond. Let's embark on a journey to explore how Copilot elevates your workflow in some of the most common applications:

Word:

Inspired Brainstorming: Struggling to ignite your writing process? Copilot steps in with prompts and suggestions based on your initial text or chosen topic. From crafting formal reports to composing casual emails, it offers diverse creative writing styles to kickstart your content creation journey.

Efficient Research and Summarization: Amidst a sea of information, Copilot comes to the rescue by scanning your research materials and distilling them into concise summaries, saving you precious time and effort.

Grammar and Style Assistance: Unsure about grammar or sentence structure? Copilot acts as your virtual editor, pinpointing potential errors and offering suggestions for clarity and conciseness, ensuring your writing shines with professionalism.

Excel:

Insightful Data Analysis: Drowning in spreadsheets? Copilot dives deep into your data, uncovering trends and patterns, and presenting them in visually compelling charts and visualizations. It even suggests relevant formulas and functions to simplify complex calculations.

Automated Formatting and Reporting: Say goodbye to repetitive formatting tasks! Copilot learns from your past actions and automates formatting styles for tables and charts, saving time and ensuring consistency across your spreadsheets.

Predictive Modeling and Forecasting: Need to foresee future trends? Copilot analyzes historical data, providing insights into potential future outcomes, empowering you to make informed decisions.

Teams:

Effortless Meeting Management: Lost in a labyrinth of meeting notes? Copilot automatically transcribes meetings, highlighting key points and action items, ensuring clarity and accountability for all participants.

Streamlined Meeting Summarization: Overwhelmed by lengthy meeting agendas? Copilot generates concise summaries of discussions, capturing key decisions and follow-up tasks, facilitating seamless communication within your team.

Smart Responses: Stuck for words in a team chat? Copilot analyzes the conversation context and suggests relevant responses, saving time and effort while promoting effective communication.

Beyond the Suite: Expanding Copilot's Influence

While Microsoft 365 applications showcase its prowess, Copilot's impact extends further. Its language analysis capabilities open doors to integration with other applications like project management tools and email platforms. Imagine receiving email summaries or automatically generating task lists based on your communication.

Unleashing the Full Potential

By embracing Copilot's diverse functionalities, you unlock the key to enhanced productivity, regardless of your profession. Remember, Copilot is a companion, not a substitute for your skills and creativity. Its role is to streamline workflows, automate mundane tasks, and offer insightful suggestions, enhancing your efficiency as you navigate the dynamic landscape of modern work. As you delve deeper into its capabilities, Copilot becomes your trusted ally, guiding you towards greater productivity and success.

Microsoft Copilot has transformed coding by acting as an intelligent assistant, offering real-time suggestions and streamlining workflows. But did you know you can personalize Copilot to further enhance your productivity? By harnessing its customization options, you can transform it into an extension of your coding style and preferences.

Fine-Tuning the Suggestions Engine:

Copilot's suggestions are built upon its understanding of your coding context. However, you can refine this understanding by specifying the programming language and framework you're working with. This ensures Copilot suggests code snippets relevant to the syntax and functionalities specific to your chosen environment.

Furthermore, you can define your preferred code style. This includes aspects like indentation, spacing, and naming conventions. By aligning

Copilot's suggestions with your established style, you can maintain code consistency and reduce the need for post-coding edits.

Tailoring the Suggestion Level:

Copilot offers flexibility in the scope of its suggestions. You can choose the level of detail you find most helpful. If you prefer complete functionality or class definitions, Copilot can handle that. Conversely, if you prefer more granular suggestions for smaller code segments, you can adjust the settings accordingly. This level of control allows you to tailor Copilot's assistance to your specific needs and coding habits.

Beyond Basic Settings: Advanced Customization

Copilot offers more than just language and style preferences. You can delve deeper and create custom configurations based on your specific projects and coding tasks. Here are some additional options for advanced users:

User Code Exclusions: Exclude specific code sections or files from Copilot's analysis. This is useful for maintaining complete control over sensitive code or sections with unique coding styles.

Customizable Keyboard Shortcuts: Assign keyboard shortcuts for frequently used actions, further streamlining your workflow and reducing reliance on the mouse.

Integration with External Tools: Integrate Copilot with other development tools you use, such as code linters or testing frameworks. This allows Copilot to leverage additional information from these tools, potentially leading to even more relevant and accurate suggestions.

Unlocking the Full Potential of Copilot:

By customizing Copilot, you gain a unique advantage: a coding assistant that understands your individual preferences and seamlessly integrates into your development process. This personalized experience can lead to significant benefits:

Increased Efficiency: Tailored suggestions can significantly reduce the time spent on repetitive tasks, freeing you to focus on the creative aspects of coding.

Reduced Errors: Adherence to your preferred coding style through Copilot's suggestions can minimize errors and inconsistencies in your code.

Enhanced Learning: Exposure to different code snippets and suggestions can broaden your coding knowledge and introduce you to new techniques and best practices.

Remember, personalization is an ongoing process. As your coding skills and project requirements evolve, so too should your Copilot settings. By regularly revisiting and adjusting the options, you can ensure your AI coding partner continues to provide the most effective assistance for all your coding endeavors.

Customizing keyboard shortcuts and preferences

Microsoft Copilot is a powerful AI tool designed to streamline the coding process by offering real-time suggestions and automating repetitive tasks. However, to truly unlock its full potential and enhance your workflow, customizing the keyboard shortcuts and preferences to suit your individual needs is crucial.

Why Customize?

The default settings might not always match your preferred way of working. By customizing these aspects, you can:

Boost efficiency: Optimize your workflow by assigning convenient shortcuts to frequently used Copilot functions, minimizing the need to navigate menus or use the mouse.

Enhance comfort: Align the keyboard shortcuts with your existing coding habits and preferences, creating a more intuitive and comfortable experience.

Maximize control: Tailor Copilot's behavior to your specific coding style, ensuring its suggestions align with your coding standards and preferences.

Exploring Customization Options:

The specific options available for customization may vary slightly depending on the application you're using Copilot with. However, here are some common areas you can personalize:

1. Keyboard Shortcuts:

Triggering suggestions: Assign a keyboard shortcut to instantly activate Copilot's suggestion window, allowing you to quickly access code suggestions without interrupting your coding flow.

Accepting and rejecting suggestions: Set dedicated shortcuts for accepting or rejecting suggested code snippets. This allows for faster iteration and avoids the need to use the mouse or navigate through menus.

Navigating suggestions: Customize shortcuts for moving between different suggested code options, enabling you to quickly explore various possibilities and select the most suitable one.

2. User Preferences:

Language and framework: Specify the primary programming language and framework you're working with. This helps Copilot tailor its suggestions to the specific syntax and conventions used in that particular language and framework.

Code style: Define your preferred coding style, including indentation, spacing, and naming conventions. This ensures that Copilot's suggestions adhere to your coding standards and maintain code consistency.

Suggestion level: Choose the level of detail you desire in the suggestions. Options may include complete function or class definitions, code snippets for specific lines, or even variable names. Balancing this level allows you to find a sweet spot between receiving comprehensive suggestions and maintaining control over the code you write.

Taking Control: How to Customize

The steps to customize Copilot's settings typically involve accessing your preferred code editor's settings or preferences menu. Here's a general process to guide you:

1. Access the settings menu: Locate the settings or preferences menu within your code editor. This may be found under the "File" menu or through a dedicated settings icon.

2. Navigate to Copilot settings: Look for a section or category dedicated to Copilot settings. This might be named "Copilot," "AI Assistant," or something similar.

3. Explore customization options: Within the Copilot settings, you'll find options for customizing keyboard shortcuts and user preferences. Each option should have clear instructions or descriptions, allowing you to understand what it affects.

4. Modify settings: Choose the desired options or type in your preferred keyboard shortcuts. Remember to save any changes made by clicking the "Save" or "Apply" button.

A Note on Best Practices:

Start small: Begin with customizing a few key shortcuts that will significantly impact your workflow. Gradually add more as you become comfortable with the changes.

Consistency is key: Maintain consistent keyboard shortcuts across different applications and coding projects. This helps build muscle memory and reduces mental strain when switching between tools.

Experiment and explore: Don't be afraid to try different settings and keyboard shortcuts to discover the configuration that best suits your needs.

By taking the time to customize Copilot's keyboard shortcuts and preferences, you can transform it from a helpful tool to a seamless extension of your coding environment. This personalized approach will enhance your efficiency, comfort, and ultimately, your enjoyment of the coding process.

Integrating Copilot with other development tools and extensions

Prepare to supercharge your coding prowess by seamlessly integrating Microsoft Copilot with your trusted development tools. While Copilot shines on its own, its true potential emerges when united with complementary extensions and platforms. Together, they form a symphony of efficiency, custom-tailored to amplify your coding journey.

Forging Synergies: Essential Integrations for Optimal Efficiency

Embark on a journey of discovery as we unveil the key integrations that can elevate your Copilot experience:

1. Code Editors and IDEs:

Visual Studio Code (VS Code): Embrace the dedicated Copilot extension within VS Code, delivering intuitive code suggestions and enabling immersive "Copilot Chat" functionality for complex tasks. Customize keyboard shortcuts and settings to orchestrate a harmonious Copilot workflow tailored to your preferences.

Alternative Editors: While official extensions may not grace every editor, a vibrant community ensures Copilot's presence in popular options like IntelliJ IDEA and Sublime Text through community-driven plugins, each offering unique functionalities to enrich your coding experience.

2. Version Control Systems (VCS):

Git Integration: Merge the collaborative powers of Git and Copilot, employing browser extensions to highlight code sections in need of review. Let Copilot guide your commit messages, ensuring clarity and conciseness in your version control endeavors.

3. Testing Frameworks:

Unit Testing: Embrace the synergy between Copilot and testing frameworks like Jest and Unknit, leveraging plugins to generate relevant unit test cases effortlessly. Streamline your testing process, ensuring robust code quality and stability.

4. Documentation Tools:

API Documentation: Seamlessly integrate Copilot with Swagger and Postman to automate API documentation creation. Say goodbye to manual documentation efforts, as Copilot extracts insights from your code comments and function definitions, ensuring consistency and accuracy.

5. Linters and Formatters:

Code Style Harmony: Enforce code consistency with Copilot's integration with Slint and Prettier. Maintain code cleanliness and readability effortlessly, safeguarding against errors and enhancing project maintainability.

Unveiling Advanced Possibilities

Venture beyond conventional integrations and explore the realm of custom extensions and scripts. With coding prowess, craft bespoke solutions that interact with Copilot in novel ways, tailored precisely to your project's needs and your coding preferences.

Remember: Ensure compatibility with Copilot, your chosen tools, and your operating system when exploring integrations. Start with a select few integrations and expand gradually as you familiarize yourself with their benefits and intricacies.

By harmonizing Copilot with your development ecosystem, you sculpt a refined environment conducive to productivity and satisfaction. Unleash the potential of integrations, experiment with diverse combinations, and witness how Copilot elevates your coding journey to new heights of efficiency and creativity.

Managing privacy and security settings

Welcome to the realm of Microsoft Copilot, where coding prowess meets AI ingenuity. As you embark on your coding odyssey with this revolutionary assistant, it's natural to ponder the intricacies of privacy and security. Fear not, for we shall unravel the mysteries surrounding data handling and empower you to navigate this digital landscape with confidence and clarity.

Deciphering Data Collection and Utilization:

Within the realm of Copilot, data flows through various channels, encompassing:

Your Code Creations: Every stroke of your keyboard, every line you craft or revise within your development sanctum, contributes to Copilot's repository.

Prompt and Response Dynamics: Engage Copilot in code-generation dialogues, and both your inquiries and Copilot's responses become part of the data tapestry.

User Identity Insights: While Copilot may gather user information such as names and affiliations, rest assured, these details remain detached from specific code snippets or interactions.

Crucially, all data embraced by Copilot undergoes a metamorphosis into anonymity. Stripped of personal identifiers, it merges into a vast sea of code, indistinguishable and untraceable. Moreover, Copilot abstains from utilizing this data to train its AI models, maintaining a clear separation between user data and algorithmic evolution.

Transparency and Data Custodianship:

At the heart of Microsoft's ethos lies a commitment to transparency and user sovereignty over data. Here's how you can steer your privacy ship amidst the Copilot waves:

Navigating the Microsoft Privacy Statement: Dive into the depths of Microsoft's Privacy Statement, a compass guiding you through the intricacies of data stewardship across their array of offerings, including Copilot.

Data Voyage Documentation: Chart a course to access and export the data Copilot has amassed during your coding expeditions. Armed with this knowledge, you hold the helm of your data destiny.

Toggling Data Collection: Though not the preferred course for optimal Copilot functionality, you retain the option to opt out of data collection. However, be mindful that this may dim the beacon of Copilot's personalized insights and learning capabilities.

Elevating Security:

Beyond the veil of anonymity lies the bastion of security, shielding your data from prying eyes. Here's how to fortify your defenses within the Copilot realm:

Guardian of Strong Authentication: Fortify your Microsoft account with a robust password, erecting a formidable barrier against unauthorized access to Copilot and its kin.

Sentinel of Two-Factor Authentication (2FA): Enlist the aid of 2FA to fortify your Microsoft account further, adding an impenetrable layer of security to your data fortress.

Vigilant Updates: Keep the gates of your operating system and development environment fortified with timely security updates, ensuring no chinks in your armor remain unaddressed.

Prudent Code Sharing: Exercise caution when sharing code with Copilot, especially if it conceals sensitive information. While anonymized, vigilance is the cornerstone when safeguarding confidential or proprietary code.

Harmonizing Functionality and Security:

As you traverse the Copilot landscape, remember to maintain equilibrium between functionality and security.

By comprehending the anonymization process, wielding data access tools, and implementing robust security measures, you can harness Copilot's capabilities while retaining sovereignty over your data kingdom. In this intricate dance of functionality and security, striking the perfect balance ensures a seamless coding voyage with Copilot as your trusted guide.

Ah, the marvels of technology! Yet, amidst the digital wonderland, lurk the occasional gremlins, ready to disrupt our digital journey. Fear not, for we embark on a quest to tame these technical woes, armed with knowledge and resilience. Join us as we unveil the secrets to troubleshooting common issues and restoring serenity to your digital domain.

The Art of Observation: Deciphering the Puzzle

Before we dive into solutions, let us first unravel the mystery at hand. Take a moment to observe and gather clues:

Recall the Scene: What were you doing when the glitch reared its head? Understanding the context can unveil potential triggers.

Decode the Message: Ah, the cryptic error messages! What tale do they tell? These messages often hold the key to unlocking the puzzle.

Inspect Recent Changes: Has anything altered in your digital realm recently? Updates or new installations may hold the key to the enigma.

Unmasking the Troublemaker: Common Culprits in the Digital Realm

Armed with insights, let us now unveil the perpetrators lurking in the shadows:

Software Bugs: The elusive bugs, hidden within the code, can wreak havoc on your digital sanctuary.

Hardware Gremlins: Beware the whispers of faulty hardware, from a mischievous RAM to a temperamental hard drive.

Outdated Software: The passage of time can render software obsolete, leading to compatibility woes and security breaches.

Connectivity Quandaries: Ah, the tangled web of connectivity! A faltering internet connection can disrupt the digital flow.

Configuration Conundrums: Misconfigured settings, the silent saboteurs, can sow chaos within your digital realm.

Embracing Action: Strategies for Navigating the Digital Labyrinth

With the foes unmasked, let us embark on our quest for resolution:

Consult the Scrolls: Delve into the depths of software documentation, where ancient wisdom awaits. Here, you may find answers to your digital conundrum.

Venture into the Archives: The vast expanse of the internet holds a treasure trove of knowledge. Seek solace in online forums and communities, where fellow travelers share tales of triumph over technical tribulations.

Invoke the Restart Ritual: Ah, the simple yet potent act of restarting! Often, this incantation can banish the digital demons and restore harmony.

Chase the Updates: Stay vigilant in your pursuit of updates, for they hold the promise of renewal and fortification against the forces of chaos.

Probe the Connections: Should the digital currents falter, venture forth to inspect the conduits of connectivity. A swift troubleshoot may mend the frayed threads.

Enlist the Tech Savants: When all else fails, seek the counsel of the digital sages. Technical support specialists and seasoned digital adventurers may offer guidance in your darkest hour.

Fortifying Your Digital Bastion: Building Resilience in the Digital Realm

As we conclude our quest, let us fortify our defenses against future incursions:

Hoist the Shields of Backup: Safeguard your digital treasures with regular backups, shielding them from the whims of fate.

Navigate the Web Safely: Tread cautiously in the digital wilderness, avoiding treacherous paths and dubious downloads.

Summon the Guardians: Arm your digital fortress with vigilant sentinels—antivirus and anti-malware software—to repel malevolent intruders.

Embrace the Vigil of Updates: Embrace the rhythm of updates, for they breathe life into your digital realm, fortifying its defenses against the ever-evolving threats.

Armed with these insights and strategies, you are now prepared to navigate the labyrinth of technical challenges with confidence and resilience. Remember, in the face of adversity, remain steadfast, gather your wits, and embark on your journey to digital triumph.

Identifying and resolving common errors and unexpected behavior

Welcome to the realm of Microsoft Copilot, your faithful AI coding companion. While Copilot boasts immense prowess in aiding development endeavors, even the mightiest allies can stumble upon occasional challenges. Fear not! This guide serves as your compass through the maze of Copilot errors and unexpected behaviors, ensuring a seamless journey toward coding excellence.

Deciphering the Origins of Errors:

As we embark on this quest, it's essential to understand that Copilot is a work in progress, continuously honing its skills. Thus, errors may arise from limitations in its training data or its grasp of intricate coding nuances. Additionally, external factors like software conflicts or internet connectivity hiccups can contribute to the occasional stumble.

Encountering Common Quirks:

Let's illuminate the path ahead by shedding light on some prevalent Copilot quirks and the strategies to conquer them:

1. Inaccurate Suggestions:

Scenario: Copilot offers code snippets that miss the mark or veer off course from your coding intentions.

Troubleshooting:

Precision in Prompts: Provide Copilot with clear instructions and contextual details to steer it toward your desired coding destination.

Training Data Review: Should discrepancies persist, consider exploring alternative training data sets within your Copilot settings to refine its understanding.

2. Missing or Incomplete Suggestions:

Scenario: Copilot falls silent or presents incomplete code snippets that demand manual intervention.

Troubleshooting:

Syntax Scrutiny: Ensure your code adheres to proper syntax and structure, providing Copilot with a solid foundation for accurate predictions.

Suggestion Level Adjustment: Experiment with tweaking the suggestion level settings to strike a balance between precision and comprehensiveness.

3. Unexpected Behavior:

Scenario: Copilot displays peculiar behavior, suggesting code that strays from coding standards or introduces security vulnerabilities.

Troubleshooting:

Manual Review and Testing: Exercise caution and conduct thorough testing of Copilot-generated code to ensure alignment with coding standards and security protocols.

Reporting Anomalies: Should anomalies persist, consider reporting them to Microsoft through official support channels to aid in Copilot's refinement.

Pioneering Proactive Strategies:

Beyond troubleshooting, let us fortify our defenses with proactive measures to navigate the digital terrain:

Stay Updated: Keep Copilot up to date with the latest software versions, unlocking new features and bug fixes.

Community Engagement: Forge alliances with fellow developers in online forums and communities dedicated to Copilot, sharing insights and troubleshooting tips.

Clarity in Communication: Articulate your coding intentions with precision when interacting with Copilot, empowering it to deliver accurate and tailored suggestions.

Armed with these insights and strategies, you are poised to conquer any challenges that may arise in your Copilot journey. Embrace the ever-evolving landscape of AI coding assistance, leveraging Copilot's prowess to elevate your development endeavors to new heights of excellence.

Getting help from Microsoft support and online communities

Encountering challenges while using Microsoft products or services is common, but finding the right help is key. This guide explores two primary avenues for assistance: official Microsoft support and online communities. Here's how to leverage these resources to resolve any issues you encounter.

1. Official Microsoft Support:

Microsoft offers a robust support system tailored to your needs. Here's how to access it:

Microsoft Support Website: This centralized hub provides product-specific pages, a keyword search bar, and categorized help topics.

Contacting Microsoft Support: For personalized assistance, options include:

Live Chat: Engage in real-time conversations with Microsoft support representatives.

Phone Support: Directly contact Microsoft support via phone for personalized assistance.

Email Support: Submit your query through an email form on the support website for a timely response.

2. Online Communities:

Online communities provide valuable assistance and insights from fellow users. Consider these platforms:

Microsoft Tech Community: This official forum allows users to ask questions, share knowledge, and collaborate on technical issues.

Microsoft Answers Forums: These forums cater to specific products, offering user-generated content and discussions.

Social Media Groups: Numerous social media groups dedicated to Microsoft products foster interaction and knowledge sharing.

Maximizing Your Support Experience

To make the most of both support avenues, follow these tips:

Clearly Articulate Your Issue: Be specific about the problem you're facing.

Provide Relevant Context: Include details like product version and error messages.

Utilize Search Functions: Use keywords to see if your question has already been answered.

Engage Constructively: Be respectful and professional in your interactions.

Evaluate Solutions Critically: Ensure solutions align with official recommendations from Microsoft.

Remember, seeking help is a positive step towards mastering technology. By effectively using these resources, you can overcome any challenges and enhance your Microsoft experience.

Chapter 8: Ethical Considerations and Responsible Use

In light of the fact that Microsoft Copilot is continuing to transform the landscape of coding, important issues about its ethical implications and responsible usage are constantly being raised. It is necessary to understand the possible hazards and make certain that this powerful tool is used in an ethical manner. While it is undeniable that it improves the efficiency and productivity of developers, it requires that this be done.

It is important to be aware of such biases

There are worries about the possible biases that may be present within the data that Copilot is trained on since it is trained on a vast dataset of current code. A number of different ways in which these biases might present themselves include the perpetuation of gender or racial stereotypes, in the event that the training data contains such prejudices. When Copilot makes code suggestions based on biased data, it has the potential to accidentally include such biases into the program that is designed to function.

Taking Steps to Reduce Bias:

Microsoft is taking measures to address this risk by putting into action a variety of different initiatives.

To begin, they are making an effort to broaden the scope of their training data by including code from a greater variety of authors and sources. In addition, they are working on building algorithms that are able to identify and eliminate any possible biases that may be present in the data. However, it's vital for developers to be watchful and critically examine the ideas made by Copilot, being cognizant of any biases and actively pursuing alternate solutions when required.

Combating Plagiarism:

Copilot's capacity to produce code snippets raises issues about possible plagiarism. While it's supposed to aid developers, not replace them, there's a danger of consumers mindlessly accepting and integrating Copilot's ideas without due acknowledgment. This may lead to ethical and legal difficulties, particularly when working with copyrighted code.

Promoting Responsible Use:

To guarantee appropriate usage, developers should:

Clearly comprehend the provenance of any code, even those proposed by Copilot.

Attribute any code snippets taken from other sources, including Copilot, appropriately.

Maintain a critical eye and study the ideas made by Copilot before integrating them.

Utilize Copilot as a tool to improve their own work, not as a substitute for their coding talents and creativity.

Transparency and Open Communication:

Microsoft plays a big role in supporting responsible usage via continuing work in three main areas:

Transparency: Providing users with clear and thorough information about how Copilot works, including its limits and possible biases.

Education: Offering instructional tools and tutorials to assist developers learn how to utilize Copilot legally and responsibly.

Community Engagement: Fostering open communication and engagement with the developer community to resolve problems and build best practices for ethical Copilot usage.

The Future of Ethical AI in Coding:

The ethical issues surrounding Copilot underscore the wider topic concerning responsible use of artificial intelligence (AI) in numerous domains. As AI technologies grow more powerful, it's vital to build rigorous ethical frameworks and best practices to guarantee their development and deployment correspond with human values and beliefs. By understanding possible problems and actively working towards responsible usage, we can utilize the power of AI tools like Copilot to advance the future of coding without sacrificing on ethics or creativity.

Understanding the biases and limits of Copilot

Microsoft Copilot, the AI-powered coding helper, has taken the developer world by storm. Its ability to propose appropriate code snippets and whole functions has surely enhanced efficiency and productivity for many developers. However, it's vital to note that Copilot, like any AI tool, is not without restrictions and possible biases.

The Source of Bias: Training Data Matters

Copilot's ideas are generated from its training data, a huge repository of existing code. While this data gives significant insights into prevalent coding habits, it naturally reflects the biases present in the actual world. If the training data is excessively biased towards certain libraries, frameworks, or coding styles, Copilot's recommendations may prefer such techniques, thereby restricting the range of solutions it gives. Furthermore, if the training data has historical biases in areas like gender or race, these prejudices may slowly enter into Copilot's recommendations, presenting ethical problems around fairness and representation.

Mitigating Bias: A Collaborative Effort

Recognizing these possible biases is the first step towards reducing their influence. Developers may use a critical lens when reviewing Copilot's ideas, examining alternative ways and ensuring their code matches their own beliefs and goals. Additionally, adding diverse and inclusive code to public repositories might help shape Copilot's future training data, progressively diminishing the effect of current biases. Open communication and cooperation between developers and the creators of Copilot are vital in eliminating any bias and ensuring the ethical use of this powerful technology.

Limitations: Understanding the Boundaries

While Copilot excels at recommending code snippets and executing regular tasks, it's crucial to remember that it is not a substitute for human judgment and skill. It cannot comprehend the complicated logic and general design of a project, nor can it understand the unique context and special needs of any development venture. Developers must stay in charge, leveraging Copilot as an aid to boost their productivity, not as a replacement for their critical thinking and problem-solving abilities.

Beyond the Code: Ethical Considerations

The possibility for bias and restrictions goes beyond the technical components of Copilot. Developers must be cognizant of the ethical consequences of utilizing Copilot, especially regarding:

Attribution: When adopting Copilot's advice, it's necessary to correctly credit the source and verify that the code fits with current license conditions.

Plagiarism: While Copilot's purpose is to help with the coding process, simply adopting its ideas without sufficient comprehension may lead to plagiarism. Developers should always thoroughly study and amend ideas to ensure the final code matches their own knowledge and effort.

Transparency and Explainability: Understanding the logic behind Copilot's proposals may help developers make educated choices and avoid introducing unwanted effects. While obtaining perfect transparency in AI models is hard, aiming for clear information about the limits and possible biases of Copilot is vital for responsible usage.

Copilot provides a substantial development in developer help, delivering essential support in terms of efficiency and productivity. However, it's crucial to understand and address any biases and limits to guarantee responsible and ethical usage. By being watchful and participating in open communication, developers may utilize the advantages of Copilot while limiting its limitations, eventually promoting a more inclusive and inventive future for software development.

Best practices for code credit and preventing plagiarism

In the field of software development, where cooperation and creativity thrive, ensuring appropriate code credit and preventing plagiarism are key parts of sustaining ethical and professional behavior. This not only secures the intellectual property of original producers but also creates trust and openness throughout the development community.

This book gives you with the fundamental information and methods to guarantee your code corresponds to the highest ethical standards.

Understanding Code Attribution: Giving Credit Where Credit is Due

Code attribution simply refers to the process of recognizing the source of any code snippet, function, or whole framework that isn't your own design. This may include the following:

Open-source libraries and frameworks: When employing publicly accessible open-source code in your project, it's vital to comply with the precise licensing conditions connected with that code. This sometimes entails incorporating a copy of the license inside your project and giving unambiguous credit within the code itself, often via comments or dedicated sections.

Code snippets from online resources: If you're employing code snippets available online, whether from forums, articles, or documentation, it's crucial to recognize the source and, where appropriate, give a link back to the original resource.

Colleagues' contributions: Working in a collaborative setting sometimes entails integrating code produced by colleagues. In many circumstances, providing unambiguous comments inside the code or maintaining a version control system that records authorship guarantees correct credit.

Why Attribution Matters: Beyond Legality

Beyond legal compliance, accurate code attribution is vital for various reasons:

Respecting intellectual property: It appreciates the hard work and inventiveness spent by the original author, promoting a culture of respect throughout the developer community.

Encouraging cooperation and transparency: Openly admitting borrowed code helps people to understand the basis upon which your project is built, promoting trust and collaboration.

Ensuring code quality and maintainability: By giving explicit attribution, you allow others to readily trace down the source of individual code segments, easing troubleshooting and preserving the code's integrity over time.

Avoiding Plagiarism: Maintaining Ethical Boundaries

While credit is necessary, it's as crucial to keep clear of plagiarism. Plagiarism, in the context of coding, covers the act of copying or substantially recreating someone else's code without appropriate acknowledgment, presenting it as your own. This not only breaches ethical precepts but may also have legal ramifications.

Here are some essential techniques to prevent plagiarism:

Understand the boundaries: Clearly distinguish between utilizing code snippets with appropriate citation and just copying code without recognizing the source.

Paraphrase with caution: When trying to restate old code structure or logic, ensure you preserve adequate uniqueness and avoid merely duplicating the original code's functioning without major alteration.

Prioritize understanding: Instead, then just duplicating code, attempt to comprehend the fundamental ideas and rationale behind it. This enables you to customize and integrate the idea inside your project while keeping uniqueness.

Leverage resources ethically: While internet resources and forums may be important tools, remember to utilize them responsibly. Avoid directly copying code from these sources without credit and actively seek help or modify notions rather than just repeating them verbatim.

Maintaining a Culture of Integrity: Building Trust and Collaboration

By adhering to responsible standards for code attribution and avoiding plagiarism, you help to maintaining a healthy and ethical development community. This not only protects intellectual property but also creates trust, transparency, and cooperation within the developer community. Remember, your code represents your expertise and dedication to ethical behavior. By respecting these ideals, you help to building a more collaborative and inventive environment for developers globally.

Using Copilot ethically and responsibly

Microsoft Copilot, the AI-powered coding assistance, has changed the software development world. Its ability to deliver contextually relevant code ideas has certainly enhanced efficiency and productivity for developers of all levels. However, with the emergence of such powerful technologies comes the essential obligation to utilize them ethically and responsibly.

Understanding Biases and Limitations

It's crucial to note that Copilot, like any AI technology, is not without its limits. The code recommendations it makes are dependent on the large quantity of code it's trained on, which might possibly reflect existing biases or limits inherent in that data. These biases may emerge in numerous ways, such as reinforcing gender or racial prejudices if the training data includes such biases.

Therefore, it's vital to be aware of these possible limits and use critical thinking while considering Copilot's ideas. Don't blindly accept anything it suggests. Instead, assess the proposals in the context of your code's goal and verify they accord with ethical values of inclusion and justice.

Combating Plagiarism: Attribution and Transparency

Copilot thrives on learning from existing code, which raises worries about possible plagiarism. It's vital to note that Copilot's proposals are not entire answers but rather beginning points. They should never be directly copied and pasted into your code without appropriate credit.

Always recognize the source of inspiration, particularly if a major percentage of the code stems from Copilot's ideas. This may be done by comments inside your code, noting the precise prompts utilized, or giving links to relevant sites. By preserving openness and providing credit where credit is due, you show responsible use of the technology and respect the ethical ideals of authorship.

Maintaining Control and Fostering Creativity

While Copilot provides a great help, it's crucial to remember that you, the developer, stay in charge. Don't depend completely on its ideas. Use them as a springboard for your own creativity and critical thinking. Analyze their viability, comprehend the rationale behind them, and adjust them to match your personal coding objectives.

Furthermore, avoid overdependence on Copilot for simple coding tasks. Continuously refine your own abilities and knowledge via practice and independent study. This will guarantee that you have a better grasp of programming concepts, allowing you to make educated choices about when and how to employ Copilot efficiently.

Moving Forward: A Collaborative Future for Development

Copilot indicates a paradigm change in the world of coding, giving a collaborative method were developers and AI work together. By utilizing Copilot wisely, you may exploit its advantages while limiting any pitfalls. Remember, ethical issues are not an afterthought; they are an intrinsic element of deploying this powerful instrument properly.

By adopting responsible usage of Copilot, we can encourage a future of collaborative creation, where humans and AI work hand-in-hand to produce creative and ethical solutions that benefit everyone.

Microsoft Copilot, the AI-powered coding assistance, has dramatically altered the development scene. While its technological components retain great curiosity, the ultimate evidence to its efficiency rests in the practical benefits delivered by real-world users. Let's examine intriguing case studies illustrating how Copilot supports developers across varied fields:

Case Study 1: Streamlining Efficiency in Web Development

The Challenge: Sarah, a web developer with five years of experience, found herself spending a large amount of time creating repeated boilerplate code for simple features like user login forms and data validation. This tedious chore not only impacted her productivity but also inhibited her capacity to concentrate on the distinctive and inventive features of web development.

The Copilot Solution: Sarah incorporated Copilot into her development environment. By evaluating the context of her existing code, Copilot started offering pre-written and optimized code snippets for commonly used features. This enabled Sarah to efficiently finish mundane chores without sacrificing quality, freeing her important time and mental space to concentrate on the fundamental logic and user experience of the website.

The Result: Sarah noted a considerable jump in her development pace, finishing tasks in much less time. This enhanced efficiency enabled her to take on more demanding duties and engage more actively to ideation and design debates, eventually leading to the establishment of a more interesting and user-friendly website.

Case Study 2: Bridging the Gap for Aspiring Data Scientists

The Challenge: Mark, a recent graduate with a love for data science, found challenges understanding and using advanced data analysis methods. While he grasped the theoretical notions, converting them into actual code proved tough. This learning curve impeded his ability to obtain hands-on experience and expand his portfolio.

The Copilot Solution: Mark included Copilot into his learning process. As he put out code for data cleaning, manipulation, and analysis chores, Copilot made pertinent ideas based on its grasp of data science libraries and common methods. This not only saved him time spent hunting for code snippets but also gave useful insights into alternative methods and best practices.

The Result: With Copilot's support, Mark was able to create and run sophisticated data analysis code with more confidence and speed. This enabled him to go deeper into complex themes, experiment with numerous methodologies, and create a solid foundation in data science. Furthermore, the quality and effectiveness of his code helped him secure his first professional data science employment.

Case Study 3: Boosting Innovation in Enterprise Software Development

The Challenge: A big software development team at a financial institution faced the ongoing pressure to offer new features and functions while preserving the reliability and security of their core platform. Balancing creativity with code quality and adherence to established practices proved tough.

The Copilot Solution: The development team carefully included Copilot into their process. While not replacing the vital human aspect of code review and quality assurance, Copilot acted as a helpful tool for recommending efficient implementations, spotting possible problems, and verifying adherence to coding standards. This enabled developers to concentrate on the creative parts of new innovations, certain that the underlying code remained stable and safe.

The Result: By exploiting Copilot's capabilities, the development team realized a considerable gain in both development speed and code quality. They were able to offer new features quicker, with fewer defects and greater maintainability. This not only increased internal productivity but also boosted the overall user experience for the financial institution's customers.

These case studies highlight the different ways in which Copilot supports developers across various skill levels and disciplines. From reducing everyday operations to promoting learning and fostering creativity, Copilot serves as a crucial tool for boosting the skills and efficiency of the contemporary developer.

Exploring real-world examples of how developers utilize Copilot

Microsoft Copilot has fast become a game-changer for developers of all levels. This revolutionary AI technology operates as a coding assistant, giving advice and automating repetitive chores to expedite the development process. But how are developers really utilizing Copilot in the real world? Let's investigate some actual instances across different code scenarios:

1. Accelerating Web Development:

Front-end engineers generally spend a large amount of time writing HTML, CSS, and JavaScript code. Copilot excels in this area by making recommendations for

Completing common HTML elements and attributes: From fundamental structures like `<div>` and `<p>` tags to more complicated components like forms and navigation bars, Copilot can help developers rapidly design the needed UI elements.

Generating CSS styles: Whether you require simple styling for text components or more complicated layouts, Copilot can recommend applicable CSS properties and values, saving you time writing repeated code.

Automating repetitive JavaScript tasks: Tasks like DOM manipulation, event handling, and AJAX requests may be simplified using Copilot's recommendation capabilities.

2. Streamlining Data Analysis Tasks:

Data analysts and scientists commonly deal with complicated libraries and frameworks like Python's Pandas and NumPy. Copilot may give important support in this arena by:

Completing data manipulation functions: From filtering and sorting data to conducting computations and transformations, Copilot may recommend applicable functions and syntax particular to the libraries being used.

Generating code for data visualization: When constructing charts and graphs using libraries like Matplotlib or Seaborn, Copilot may recommend code snippets to build certain chart types depending on the data and intended display.

Automating data cleaning tasks: Cleaning and processing dirty data sets sometimes includes repeated processes. Copilot may recommend code to handle missing values, data type conversions, and other typical cleaning activities.

3. Simplifying Mobile App Development:

Whether you're creating native apps or cross-platform applications using frameworks like React Native or Flutter, Copilot may be a significant asset:

Completing UI components for mobile apps: Similar to web development, Copilot may recommend code for constructing common UI elements unique to mobile app frameworks.

Generating code for device-specific functionalities: Tasks like accessing sensors, controlling user gestures, and regulating device orientation may be eased using Copilot's ability to provide suitable code snippets.

Automating user interface logic: Implementing user interactions inside the app, such as button clicks and form submissions, may be expedited using Copilot's code completion tools.

4. Enhancing API Integration:

Integrating external APIs into your program generally entails complicated code for authentication, data collecting, and error handling. Copilot proves beneficial by:

Suggesting code for API calls: Based on the target API and the required functionality, Copilot may recommend code snippets for initiating HTTP requests, managing various response formats, and parsing data.

Automating error handling: Implementing solid error handling methods may be laborious. Copilot may recommend code to handle probable problems during API interactions, making your code more durable.

Generating documentation for API calls: While integrating APIs, creating documentation for your own code might be vital. Copilot may propose comments and explanations depending on the API calls you're using, improving in code readability and maintainability.

5. Boosting Overall Development Efficiency:

Beyond particular instances, Copilot provides generic advantages that apply across numerous development scenarios:

Automating boilerplate code: Repetitive work like creating fundamental function structures, variable declarations, and typical code patterns may be automated using Copilot's recommendations, freeing up your time for more vital tasks.

Suggesting unit tests: As you write code, Copilot may recommend appropriate code snippets to construct unit tests, assuring the quality and dependability of your work.

Providing code style and formatting suggestions: Maintaining consistent coding style may be tough. Copilot may aid by recommending code formatting and style improvements depending on your selected coding standards.

This insight into real-world applications highlights the adaptability and promise of Copilot. As developers continue to explore its potential, we can anticipate even more novel use cases and breakthroughs in the future of coding help.

Learning from best practices and attaining particular objectives using Copilot

Microsoft Copilot has emerged as a game-changer for developers, giving an AI-powered assistant that simplifies processes and enables them to reach their coding objectives. But beyond the initial enthusiasm, leveraging Copilot's full potential involves knowing how to leverage proven practices and personalize it to particular purposes. This detailed tutorial looks into these key features, allowing you to unleash Copilot's actual worth and boost your coding adventure.

Learning from the Masters: Embracing Best Practices

Developing competence in any subject includes learning from those who succeed. The same idea applies to employing Copilot efficiently. Here are essential behaviors followed by successful users:

Craft Clear and Concise Prompts: The cornerstone for excellent Copilot recommendations depends in delivering clear and unambiguous cues. This implies properly expressing the expected functionality or code behavior, using correct language and appropriate terms. The more explicit your request, the more focused and beneficial Copilot's recommendations will be.

Embrace Experimentation: Don't be scared to experiment with new prompts and techniques. Observe how Copilot reacts to differences in the way you express your requests. This experimentation helps you to explore and enhance your communication style with Copilot, leading to more successful conversation.

Actively Review and Refine: Copilot's ideas are a starting point, not a completed result.

Always critically analyze the proposed code, ensuring it conforms with your coding standards, best practices, and overall project needs. Don't hesitate to change or reject proposals that don't match your expectations.

Seek Continuous Learning: The world of technology is always growing, and Copilot's capabilities are no exception. Actively educate yourself on new features, upgrades, and best practices around Copilot. This constant learning guarantees you can use the tool's full potential as it develops and improves.

Tailoring Copilot to Your Goals: Achieving Specific Objectives

Copilot's adaptability enables it to accommodate to varied development objectives. Here's how to maximize its utilization for various purposes:

Boosting Productivity: Leverage Copilot for activities like automating repetitive code blocks, producing boilerplate code, and recommending pertinent function definitions. This frees you to focus your mental resources to the more creative and strategic areas of coding, thereby expediting your growth process.

Enhancing Code Quality: Copilot may assist spot possible problems and recommend alternate techniques that comply to best standards. Its ability to learn your coding style and preferences further assures that the produced code complies with your coding standards, leading to cleaner, more maintainable projects.

Expanding Knowledge Base: Working with Copilot exposes you to new coding styles and problem-solving approaches. This ongoing exposure may widen your knowledge base and boost your general coding abilities, supporting long-term growth and development.

Sparking New Ideas: Sometimes, the most inventive answers originate from unexpected sources. Copilot's comments, although not necessarily the ultimate answer, may serve as a platform for fresh ideas and methods. Embrace the unexpected and embrace Copilot's suggestions as a springboard for innovative problem-solving.

By implementing these best practices and adapting Copilot to your unique aims, you can convert it from a useful tool into a strong ally in your development path. Remember, Copilot exists to compliment your talents, not replace them. By actively interacting with the tool, improving your prompts, and continually learning, you may utilize its possibilities to become a more efficient, productive, and inventive developer.

Conclusion

As you reach the last words of this book, you've ideally obtained a complete grasp of Microsoft Copilot and its potential to alter your development method. Whether you're a seasoned developer trying to optimize your workflow or a beginner ready to continue on your coding adventure, Copilot provides a crucial ally in this ever-evolving sector. Remember, Copilot is not a magic wand that creates flawless code for you. It's a strong tool that, when utilized well, can boost your productivity, improve code quality, and stimulate innovation. The key lies in knowing its strengths and limits, customizing it to your personal requirements, and continually learning from the experiences of others.

As the world of software development continues to change, so too will Copilot. Staying connected with the thriving community, learning new features, and actively contributing to the knowledge base will guarantee you stay at the forefront of this amazing technology. Before we part ways, we want to convey our heartfelt thanks for taking the time to examine this book. Your commitment to learn and invest in your coding abilities is impressive. We hope this book has provided you with the knowledge and confidence to uncover the full potential of Microsoft Copilot and raise your development journey to new heights.

Remember, the coding world is yours to explore and shape. Embrace the power of Copilot, continue learning, and never stop pushing the frontiers of innovation. The future of software development is bright, and with Copilot by your side, you're well-equipped to contribute to its brilliance.

Thank you, and happy coding!

www.ingramcontent.com/pod-product-compliance
Lightning Source LLC
Chambersburg PA
CBHW071138050326
40690CB00008B/1495